THE LITTLE GUIDE TO

# LEAVES

# THE LITTLE GUIDE TO
# LEAVES

Illustrations
by Tom Frost

Words by
Alison Davies

**quadrille**

# Introduction

Look at any plant or tree, any densely wooded glade, and your vision will be stirred by a riot of colour and texture. You'll see a variety of shapes, some curved or roughly jagged with sharp little teeth or bustling feather-like fronds, others spectacularly uniform, in perfect symmetry as if sketched by a great master.

The beautiful flesh upon the skeletal landscape of any plant or tree is the leaves, adding character and so much more as the prints in this book illustrate. Each leaf is unique, whether delicately patterned or tribal in its hue, and it's not just a visual feast that it provides; there's usually a story behind it – a reason why it curves or leans a certain way, a narrative to explain the deeper meaning and how the ancients saw it as a gift of nature. From the poisonous Ivy, whose toxic foliage was considered a symbol of intellectual prowess by the ancient Romans, to the striking Swiss Cheese Plant with leaves that stretch and tear in a bid to catch the sun's rays, this book offers up some of the finest specimens from around the world. The intricately detailed images assist in identifying the plant or tree and a combination of fascinating facts and folklore helps you understand the power of nature and the impact of an ever-changing environment. The Spotter's Guide at the back of the book is quick and easy to navigate, with all the key points that you'll need for your adventures with flora. Whether you're an avid fan of nature rambles or a pure beginner, this book is the perfect accompaniment.

Open the pages, delve into the undergrowth and let Mother Nature reveal her leafy extravaganza!

*Every leaf speaks bliss to me,*
*fluttering from the autumn tree.*

EMILY BRONTË

# Sycamore

*Acer pseudoplatanus*

**FAMILY NAME** Sapindaceae

**CHARACTERISTICS** Leaves measure 7 to 16cm (3 to 6in) and have 5 lobes

**HABITAT** Woodlands and urban areas; can also be found by the coast

**DISTRIBUTION** Most of central and southern Europe; has been introduced to the UK, Belgium, the Netherlands, Scandinavia, New Zealand and North and South America

**FLOWERS AND FRUIT** The flowers hang in spikes and are green-yellow in colour. Once pollinated, female flowers turn into 'winged' fruits called samaras

The wood from the Sycamore tree is commonly used to craft the backs, necks and scrolls of violins. The timber is strong with a fine grain, which also makes it ideal for use in furniture. It was first introduced to the UK in the 17th century, but its reputation goes back much further. Its North American cousins, which grow to mammoth proportions, were called 'ghosts of the forest' by the Native Americans who considered them a tree of magic and mystery. In Montgomeryshire, Wales, it was thought that if you planted a Sycamore tree it would keep the fairies at bay and stop them from spoiling the milk.

# Silver Maple

*Acer saccharinum*

**FAMILY NAME** Sapindaceae
**CHARACTERISTICS** Leaves with 5 deep, serrated lobes,
up to 15cm (6in) long
**HABITAT** Most commonly grows along waterways and in wetlands
**DISTRIBUTION** North-eastern United States
**FLOWERS AND FRUIT** Small, reddish flowers appear before the leaves
in early spring. Winged fruits, called samaras, contain a single seed

Sometimes called the Water or Swamp Maple because
of its preference for damp, watery areas, the tree was
associated with longevity by the Native American
Indians. They used its bark in medicines, and to
make tools and furniture. The leaves have a silvery
underside that is often exposed by the breeze, and in
autumn they can turn from a pale yellow to a burnt
orange shade. A fast grower, this tree is often planted
along streets and in urban developments.

# Horse Chestnut

*Aesculus hippocastanum*

**FAMILY NAME** Hippocastanaceae

**CHARACTERISTICS** 5 to 7 toothed leaflets radiate from a
central stem; each leaflet is approximately 25cm (10in) long

**HABITAT** Parks, gardens, streets; thrives in most soil types

**DISTRIBUTION** Europe, Asia, North America

**FLOWERS AND FRUIT** Large, upright clusters of white
and pink flowers in spring; once pollinated they turn into
spiky, green husks each containing a rich, brown conker

Introduced into the UK from Turkey in the 16th century, Horse
Chestnut sustains a wide variety of wildlife – flowers provide
nectar for many insects, especially bees; caterpillars feed on its
leaves; and many mammals eat conkers. In Greek mythology, the
chestnut is associated with Zeus, the king of the gods, and with
fertility, abundance and good fortune. Today, this tree provides the
essential part of a popular British children's game called 'conkers'.
The seed is threaded onto string so that players can swing them
against each other and knock out their opponent's conker.

# Elephant's Ear

*Alocasia × amazonica*

**FAMILY NAME** Araceae

**CHARACTERISTICS** Arrow-shaped leaves with wavy edges and conspicuous veins and purple undersides, up to 30cm (12in) long

**HABITAT** Gardens and humid environments

**DISTRIBUTION** This plant is a hybrid originally bred from Asian parents in Florida, USA

**FLOWERS AND FRUIT** Greenish yellow boat-shaped flowers, followed by red-orange fruit

Despite its exotic name, this plant isn't from the Amazon and does not grow naturally in rainforests. It's named after the nursery in Florida where it was first bred. Also known as the African Mask and the Jewel Alocasia, this pretty shrub is a popular choice for verandas and gardens and can be grown indoors at the right temperature. All parts of the plant contain irritant calcium oxalate crystals that are extremely toxic and produce a stinging and swelling effect on mucous membranes if ingested.

# Asparagus Fern

*Asparagus setaceus*

**FAMILY NAME** Asparagaceae
**CHARACTERISTICS** Up to 15 leaf-like cladodes,
7mm (¼in) long, cover each stem
**HABITAT** Forests and coastal scrub areas
**DISTRIBUTION** Native to Southern Africa
(has become an invasive weed in Australia)
**FRUITS AND FLOWERS** Green-white bell-shaped flowers,
followed by small, green toxic berries that blacken with age

This ornamental-looking but invasive plant is also known as the Common Asparagus Fern, Lace Fern and sometimes the Bride's Bouquet Fern, probably because of the soft fern-like foliage used to fill out floral arrangements. Swift to grow, this bushy evergreen perennial herb is not a true fern. It has spiny stems that tend to extend between 3 and 6 metres (10 and 20 feet) in height. Flattened shoots, known as cladodes, create the appearance of leaves, from which the flowers and fruits grow.

# Begonia

*Begonia maculata* 'Wightii'

**FAMILY NAME** Begoniaceae

**CHARACTERISTICS** Shaped like angel wings, glossy,
dark green with silvery-white spots and pink undersides

**HABITAT** Tropical rainforests

**DISTRIBUTION** Native to Brazil

**FRUITS AND FLOWERS** Clusters of white flowers
appearing late winter into spring

This tender, tropical, evergreen perennial's favourite
growing spot would be in a bright position where
it's exposed to the sunshine but avoids the intense,
hot afternoon sun. With its distinctive, speckled
bat-wing-shaped leaves, it has a number of other
names including Polka Dot Angel Wing Begonia or
Wight's Spotted Begonia. The leaves also have a
ruffled edge and an eye-catching red/pink underside.
Its stems resemble bamboo canes.

# Begonia Rex

*Begonia rex*

**FAMILY NAME** Begoniaceae

**CHARACTERISTICS** Large, ovate and metallic green leaves, with a silver zone on the upper side and a reddish one beneath, they vary in size but can grow to 23cm (9in) long

**HABITAT** Thrives in tropical understorey

**DISTRIBUTION** Native to tropical and sub-tropical regions of India

**FLOWERS AND FRUIT** Pink flowers blooming from December to February produce fruits that are capsules full of tiny seeds

Begonia Rex, or King Begonia, is a fitting title for a plant with such eye-catching leaves. The silver markings give each leaf a regal sheen. There are many varieties with names such as 'Can Can', 'Jolly Silver', 'Spitfire' and 'Pinkpop', all equally stunning and popular as ornamental houseplants. Begonia Rex thrives in shaded, humid conditions but too much water will cause it to rot.

# Silver Birch

*Betula pendula*

**FAMILY NAME** Betulaceae

**CHARACTERISTICS** Light green fading to yellow in autumn, triangular-shaped leaves with toothed edge, to about 7cm (2¾in) long

**HABITAT** Dry woodlands, downs, heaths and gardens

**DISTRIBUTION** Europe, Siberia, Turkey, Caucasus

**FLOWERS AND FRUIT** Male catkins are yellowy brown, females short and bright green. Once pollinated, female catkins turn deep crimson. Masses of seeds are dispersed by the wind in autumn

Silver Birch leaves have been used since ancient times as a diuretic. Also known for their antiseptic properties, they were included in remedies for bladder infections and kidney stones. The tree itself is associated with the coming of spring. The Celts valued its cleansing properties and used bundles of birch twigs to drive out the spirits of the old year. This later evolved into a tradition known as 'beating the bounds'. Birches help other plants by improving soil condition – they draw nutrients up from deep underground and release them back into the soil when leaves are shed in autumn.

# Zebra Plant

*Calathea zebrina*

FAMILY NAME Marantaceae

CHARACTERISTICS Ovate leaves with dark green stripes
and purple undersides, up to approximately 38cm (15in) long

HABITAT Tropical rainforests

DISTRIBUTION Native to south-eastern Brazil

FLOWERS AND FRUIT Inconspicuous purple
or white flower bracts

Striking Calatheas come in a number of different
species, including the Peacock Plant (*C. makoyana*)
and Rattlesnake Plant (*C. insignis*). The Zebra Plant is
often mistaken for the Prayer Plant (page 62) which is
closely related but does not grow as tall. The stalks of
this plant can grow up to a metre (over 3 feet) high. Its
leaves stand away from the plant and change position
slightly in response to humidity.

# Parlour Palm

*Chamaedorea elegans*

**FAMILY NAME** Arecaceae

**CHARACTERISTICS** Evergreen pinnate leaves up
to 60cm (24in) long with up to 40 linear leaflets

**HABITAT** Rainforests

**DISTRIBUTION** Mexico and Central America

**FLOWERS AND FRUIT** Some produce clusters of
yellow and cream flowers, then cream-coloured fruit,
which turn black when fully ripe

This ornamental palm (formerly *Neanthe bella*) with
its elegant stems and appearance is popular with
florists. They use its stunning fronds in displays and
decorations because, once cut, they last up to 40 days.
A favourite houseplant since Victorian times, the
Parlour Palm is adaptable and can grow in low light
and humidity. It takes many years for it to fully mature
in a tropical environment, but it will grow to a height
of around 3 metres (10 feet).

# European Fan Palm

*Chamaerops humilis*

FAMILY NAME Arecaceae

CHARACTERISTICS Large, triangular, fan-shaped
leaves, deeply cut into linear segments, approximately
60cm (24in) wide

HABITAT Cliffs above the sea, hillsides, gorges

DISTRIBUTION Europe and north-west Africa

FLOWERS AND FRUIT Small yellow flowers on mature
plants in spring followed by small, brown, date-like fruits

This bushy, evergreen shrub usually has several
stems coming from the same base that carry
fan-shaped fronds. These are cut almost up to
the stalk, giving them a sword-like appearance.
Also called the Mediterranean Dwarf Palm or
Dwarf Fan Palm because of its stumpy size, this
palm is incredibly resilient, often flourishing in
extreme conditions on sandy or rocky ground.

# Common Hawthorn

*Crataegus monogyna*

**FAMILY NAME** Rosaceae
**CHARACTERISTICS** Glossy, deeply lobed leaves
approximately 6cm (2½in) long
**HABITAT** Woodland, hedgerows and gardens
**DISTRIBUTION** Europe
**FLOWERS AND FRUIT** Pretty white or pink flowers,
which develop into dark-red berries known as 'haws'

Also known as the May Tree after the month in which it blooms,
the Common Hawthorn has long been associated with faeries.
The Celts believed that the tree was inhabited by fey folk. Leaves
were often eaten or made into a potion, along with the flowers,
to stabilize blood pressure. During medieval times the tree had a
more sinister reputation, thanks to the blossom, which smelled like
the Great Plague; scientists have since discovered that a chemical
present in the blossom is also associated with rotting flesh. Hugely
valuable for wildlife, it can provide food for hundreds of insect
species and many birds and small mammals.

# Sago Palm

*Cycas revoluta*

FAMILY NAME Cycadaceae

CHARACTERISTICS Large, glossy, deep-green leaves are around
90cm (36in) long, with many needle-like leaflets

HABITAT Coasts, hillsides and sparse forests

DISTRIBUTION Native to southern Japan and the Ryukyu Islands

FLOWERS AND FRUIT Male and female flowers
are borne on separate plants

This primitive plant dates back to the age of the
dinosaurs, around 200 million years ago. It comes
from one of the oldest plant families still thriving
today, the cycads. Closely related to conifers, but with
the appearance of a palm, it's also known as the King
Sago, Sago Cycad and Japanese Sago Palm. The
plant is highly toxic but the leaves have medicinal
properties and have been used in treatments
for cancer.

# Papyrus

*Cyperus papyrus*

FAMILY NAME Cyperaceae

CHARACTERISTICS Erect, grass-like stems with clusters
of flower spikes, around 10 to 30cm (4 to 12in) tall

HABITAT Aquatic perennial found in lakes or rivers;
it also grows in swamps and forms mats or islands

DISTRIBUTION Native in much of Africa and parts of Asia

FLOWERS AND FRUIT Greenish-brown clusters of flowers,
which eventually turn to small, brown, nut-like fruits

A tall aquatic plant, the Papyrus is often referred to as leafless, though this is not strictly true as the woody rhizome from which the plant emerges represents reduced leaves. These lush green stems gather together in dense clusters and look like feather dusters, making an ideal home for many nesting birds. The ancient Egyptians considered Papyrus the 'gift of the Nile'. They famously used this plant to make papyrus paper, although they had many other applications for it. The stems were woven into reed boats, the roots made bowls and utensils, the pith from the shoots was boiled and eaten, and the flower heads were formed into garlands and left as gifts of worship to the gods.

# Dumb Cane

*Dieffenbachia* spp.

**FAMILY NAME** Araceae

**CHARACTERISTICS** Large, heart-shaped green leaves
with white spots and flecks up to 50cm (20in) long

**HABITAT** Tropical rainforests

**DISTRIBUTION** Native to Mexico, through Central
America to northern South America and Argentina,
and on several Caribbean islands

**FLOWERS AND FRUIT** Mature plants produce
white or cream flower heads, followed by red berries

Also known as Mother-in-Law Plant and Tuftroot, the Dumb Cane
may look ornamental but it has lots of uses. As a houseplant, it
freshens the air as it eliminates significant amounts of toxins,
giving it super air-filtering properties. In Brazil, it's prized for an
altogether different ability: it's believed to keep negative energies
at bay and provide some protection against the 'evil eye' and
similar curses. For maximum effect it must be grown alongside
specially chosen herbs including Rosemary, Basil and Rue.

# Areca Palm

*Dypsis lutescens*

**FAMILY NAME** Arecaceae
**CHARACTERISTICS** Tall arched leaves, 2 to 3m
(6 to 10ft) long, with 20 to 60 pairs of leaflets
**HABITAT** Tropical and sub-tropical forests
**DISTRIBUTION** Native to Madagascar, naturalized in parts
of Central and South America and the Caribbean
**FLOWERS AND FRUIT** Panicles of yellow flowers in summer

This stately palm is also known as the Butterfly Palm because
of the way the leaves curl upwards, giving the appearance
of butterfly wings. The leaves, though primarily green with
a few dark specks at the base of the stem, are sometimes
shades of yellow and gold, which explains another popular
name for this plant, the Golden Cane Palm. This plant is
'self-cleaning', in that once the leaves turn brown they fall
away with the crown shaft. A clustering palm, it can reach
up to 12 metres (40 feet) tall when fully mature.

# Eucalyptus

*Eucalyptus globulus*

**FAMILY NAME** Myrtaceae

**CHARACTERISTICS** Young blue-green leaves are small and rounded on long, slender and pendulous stalks – up to 35cm (14in) – when mature

**HABITAT** Dry thickets, brushland, woods and gardens

**DISTRIBUTION** Native to Australia, New Guinea and Indonesia

**FLOWERS AND FRUIT** White, pink, cream, yellow or red flowers with tassels of stamens; fruits are small, cone-shaped capsules full of seeds

The name *Eucalyptus* comes from the Greek words *eu* and *kaluptos*, meaning 'well-covered', which refers to the copious stamens in the flowers shielded by an *Operculum*. It is also known as the Gum Tree. Mature leaves point downwards in a bid to conserve water and avoid direct exposure to sunlight. They're rich in eucalyptus oil which, as well as being an insecticide, is known for its medicinal properties. The Blue Mountains in New South Wales, Australia, gets its iconic name from the groves of Eucalyptus that cover the range. The oil content of the leaves produces a hazy blue mist which creates a haunting vista.

# Beech

*Fagus sylvatica*

**FAMILY NAME** Fagaceae

**CHARACTERISTICS** 4 to 9cm (1½ to 3½in) long, young leaves are lime green, turning darker with age. Oval with pointed tips and wavy edges

**HABITAT** Areas of dry, free-draining soils, especially chalk and limestone

**DISTRIBUTION** Europe, from southern Sweden to northern Sicily

**FLOWERS AND FRUIT** Male and female flowers grow on the same tree; male are tasselled catkins, female grow in pairs and once pollinated produce one or two beech nuts known as 'beech mast'

Beech trees are extremely long-lived and have a strong association with divination and looking into the future. In parts of 18th-century Germany, it was thought that babies were produced from a hollow Beech, rather than the more traditional route of being delivered by a stork. In ancient times, thin slices of the wood were made into tablets to write on, and the bark was used to make carvings, a practice that dates back to the Romans. The leaves had potent medicinal qualities, and were often used in poultices to heal skin complaints. They were also stuffed into bedding to promote a speedy recovery from illness.

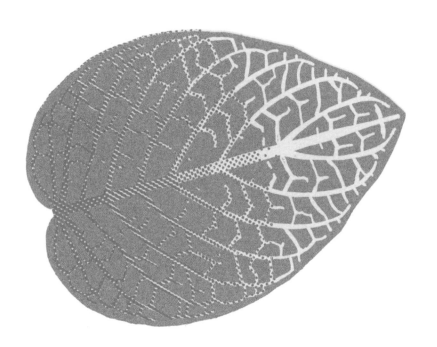

# Fittonia

*Fittonia albivenis*

**FAMILY NAME** Acanthaceae

**CHARACTERISTICS** Oval green leaves, 3 to 10cm
(1¼ to 4in) long, with a network of white to reddish veins

**HABITAT** Tropical rainforests

**DISTRIBUTION** Native to South America, mostly Peru

**FLOWERS AND FRUIT** Plants rarely flower in cultivation,
but when they do they produce small white blooms

Fittonia is a spreading, evergreen perennial with striking
foliage, growing up to 15cm (6in) tall. It is also known
as the Nerve or Mosaic Plant because of the obvious
web of veins that thread each leaf. The Machiguenga,
an indigenous people of the Amazon basin jungle
region of south-eastern Peru, once used the leaf as a
hallucinogen, claiming that it produced 'visions of the
eyeballs'. Other indigenous peoples, such as the Secoya,
use the leaves in a concoction to treat headaches.

# Ash

*Fraxinus excelsior*

**FAMILY NAME** Oleaceae

**CHARACTERISTICS** Pinnate leaves around 35cm (14in)
long bearing pairs of finely toothed leaflets

**HABITAT** Fertile, deep, well-drained soils; often dominates woodlands

**DISTRIBUTION** Europe, Asia Minor, Africa

**FLOWERS AND FRUIT** Small purple flowers appear at tips of twigs
before leaves in spring; winged fruits resemble bunches of small keys

The Ash is known for its healing properties. In British folklore, sick children were often given a teaspoon of ash sap to cure them of any ailment, and babies were passed through its boughs for this purpose. The Vikings considered the Ash sacred – their 'World Tree', also called *Yggdrasil,* was an Ash. Its roots reached down to the underworld and its branches up to the heavens. According to one legend, the god Odin hung from this tree for nine days and nights, an ordeal for which the ultimate prize was enlightenment and the wisdom to create the runic system. The Ash is a perfect wildlife habitat for many species including woodpeckers, owls and nuthatches.

# Ginkgo

*Ginkgo biloba*

**FAMILY NAME** Ginkgoaceae

**CHARACTERISTICS** Fan-shaped leaves, sometimes divided
into two lobes, 5 to 10cm (2 to 4in) long, bright green in summer,
yellow in autumn

**HABITAT** From forests to urban areas

**DISTRIBUTION** Native to Xitianmu Mountain in Zhejiang, China

**FLOWERS AND FRUIT** Male catkin-like flowers and smaller female
flowers which produce light-yellow to purplish fruits in autumn

One of the oldest trees in the world, the Ginkgo, also known
as the Maidenhair Tree in the UK, has been around for
350 million years. It is a living fossil and individual trees
can live for over a thousand years, which explains the tree's
association with longevity. In Chinese, its name means
'silver apricot' and the leaves are prized for their medicinal
qualities. It is also used in western medicine as it has been
shown to improve blood circulation to the brain and is used
in the treatment of cognitive conditions such as Alzheimer's.

# Juniper

*Juniperus communis*

**FAMILY NAME** Cupressaceae

**CHARACTERISTICS** Aromatic, grey-green, needle-like leaves, around 1cm (⅜in) long, becoming scale-like when mature

**HABITAT** Dry, open, rocky hillsides, heaths, coastal areas

**DISTRIBUTION** Widely across Northern Hemisphere

**FLOWERS AND FRUIT** Dioecious; female flowers, once pollinated, turn into blue-black, berry-like cones

The Juniper is best known for its berries which were once used by ancient Egyptians to cure tapeworm infestations; the Romans made tinctures as a remedy for stomach complaints. The Celts would burn the wood for purification and to encourage psychic visions, and in Europe the same Juniper-scented smoke was used to cast out demons. Today, the berries are most famously used to flavour gin and are responsible for its distinctive taste. They're also used in cooking to flavour sauces. Juniper trees provide food and shelter for wildlife species, such as black grouse, thrushes and many moths.

# Honey Locust

*Gleditsia triacanthos*

**FAMILY NAME** Fabaceae

**CHARACTERISTICS** Glossy, green compound leaves with paired leaflets, 15 to 20cm (6 to 8in) long, turning a brilliant yellow in autumn

**HABITAT** Adaptable to many conditions, gardens and urban areas

**DISTRIBUTION** North America

**FLOWERS AND FRUIT** Small, greenish-yellow flowers followed by clusters of long, strap-like seed pods

Often known as the Honey Locust because of the sticky pulp that comes from its pods, this tree is also sometimes called the Thorny Locust because of the prickly spines that grow on the trunk and base of its branches. Most cultivated varieties do not have thorns and are planted as ornamental specimens. The sticky, sweet pulp in its pods has a sugary taste and was used traditionally by Native Americans as a sweetener in foods and medicines. Today, it's widely used in anti-cancer medicines and to treat rheumatoid arthritis.

# Common Ivy

*Hedera helix*

**FAMILY NAME** Araliaceae

**CHARACTERISTICS** Dark green, glossy, 3–5-lobed leaves, varying in size but typically 6.5cm (2½in) long, often with obvious veining

**HABITAT** Woodland, hedgerows, gardens; thrives in shady places

**DISTRIBUTION** Throughout Europe

**FLOWERS AND FRUIT** Small, green-yellow flowers on mature plants in autumn followed by black berries in winter

This evergreen climber has a reputation for keeping evil spirits at bay. In medieval times it was considered a good omen if your home was covered in Ivy. The ancient Romans and Greeks also valued it, believing Ivy to be a symbol of intellectual achievement. Wreaths were often given as prizes in poetry competitions and for those showing athletic prowess. It is not parasitic – although it grows on trees for support, it has its own root system. All parts of the plant are toxic to humans, but Ivy is an important food source for many insects and birds.

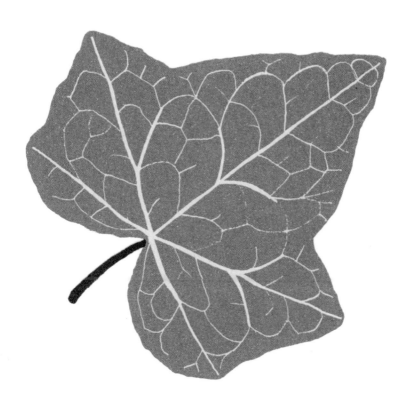

# Holly

*Ilex aquifolium*

**FAMILY NAME** Aquifoliaceae

**CHARACTERISTICS** Leathery, glossy green, oval leaves, often with sharp spines but sometimes without, approximately 6.5cm (2½in) long

**HABITAT** Lowlands to mountains; moist, fairly rich soils; woodland and gardens

**DISTRIBUTION** Europe, Western Asia, North Africa

**FLOWERS AND FRUIT** Clusters of creamy-white flowers on stems followed by shiny red berries around 1cm (⅜in) diameter

It's easy to spot Holly trees during winter when the fruit is present; being evergreen, the leaves remain a luscious, dark green hue all year round. According to folklore, Holly was known for its protective properties. Associated with Thor, the Norse god of thunder and lightning, holly was believed to prevent people from being struck by lightning if they sheltered beneath a tree. Holly berries are an important food source for many birds and small mammals in winter.

# Sweet Gum

*Liquidambar styraciflua*

**FAMILY NAME** Altingiaceae

**CHARACTERISTICS** Bright-green, shiny, star-shaped leaves with 5 or 7 sharp lobes, 10 to 15cm (4 to 6in) long, turning orange-red-purple in autumn

**HABITAT** Woodland, parks, fields, gardens

**DISTRIBUTION** Eastern North America, Mexico and Central America

**FLOWERS AND FRUIT** Pale green flowers in dense clusters; spiny fruit balls contain many tiny seeds

The Sweet Gum tree gets its name from the yellowish-brown sap that oozes from the bark when penetrated. Native Americans used this sap as chewing gum and also to treat a number of complaints including diarrhoea, feverish symptoms and skin problems. The fragrant resin is also a key ingredient in perfumes and in other medicinal products. The tree is a popular haunt for blue jays, finches, chipmunks and squirrels, which feed on the seeds.

# Tulip Tree

*Liriodendron tulipifera*

**FAMILY NAME** Magnoliaceae
**CHARACTERISTICS** Large, heart-shaped, green leaves with four lobes, up to 20cm (8in) across, turning yellow in autumn
**HABITAT** Open, damp to moist soils, forests, woods, parks and gardens
**DISTRIBUTION** Eastern North America
**FLOWERS AND FRUIT** Flowers are greenish-yellow and tulip-shaped; fruits are narrow, brown cones of many samaras

One of the tallest eastern American hardwoods, this tree stands straight and towering above the rest. Also known as the Yellow Poplar or the Whitewood, in some regions it's called the 'canoe tree' as early settlers and Native Americans would hollow out logs to make their boats. The bark is strong but pliable and often used to make furniture. It is the state tree of Kentucky, Tennessee and Indiana.

# Red-Veined Prayer Plant

*Maranta leuconeura* var. *erythroneura*

**FAMILY NAME** Marantaceae

**CHARACTERISTICS** Broad, oval green leaves with
red midrib and veins, up to 12cm (5in) long

**HABITAT** Tropical rainforests

**DISTRIBUTION** Brazil

**FLOWERS AND FRUIT** Tiny white flowers
with purple spots in summer

Also known as the Rabbit's Foot or Rabbit's Track,
this evergreen perennial has leaves that lie flat
during daylight and stand erect at night, giving the
appearance of hands clasped together in prayer. As
it unfurls in the morning it makes a gentle rustling
sound. Its intricately detailed leaves have red veins
arranged in a feather-like pattern. The leaves
sometimes have a red underside and the plants
grow in clumps, usually in well-shaded areas.

# Swiss Cheese Plant

*Monstera deliciosa*

**FAMILY NAME** Araceae
**CHARACTERISTICS** Mostly ovate, often pinnate or perforated, glossy green leaves, growing up to 90cm (36in) long
**HABITAT** Tropical rainforests
**DISTRIBUTION** Native to Central and South America
**FLOWERS AND FRUIT** White flower spathes; fruit resemble sweetcorn cobs and are edible when fully ripe

The Swiss Cheese Plant is an epiphyte with aerial roots that attach themselves to host trees which it then climbs. In its early stages, the plant has small leaves without holes, held close to the tree trunk. As it matures, the plant gets taller, reaching more patches of sunlight in the forest's canopy, and this is believed to cause the holes in the leaves. As the plant climbs higher, the leaves get bigger and develop tears that ensure that they take up more space and absorb maximum rays. Popular as a houseplant, other common names include Monster Fruit and Window Leaf.

# Sword Fern

*Nephrolepis exaltata*

**FAMILY NAME** Lomariopsidaceae

**CHARACTERISTICS** Arching, evergreen fronds,
50 to 150cm (20 to 60in) long

**HABITAT** Swamps and tropical forests

**DISTRIBUTION** Common in northern South America, Mexico,
Central America, Florida, the West Indies, Polynesia and Africa

**FLOWERS AND FRUIT** Ferns are non-flowering

An invasive plant with spreading runners, the Sword
Fern grows in shady spots beneath the jungle canopy.
Other names for this plant include the Boston or
Fishbone Fern. The sharp, sword-like fronds grow
upwards at first but begin to arch outwards as they
mature to form an elegant shape which is prized
by plant·growers. A popular houseplant, it is often
grown in hanging baskets.

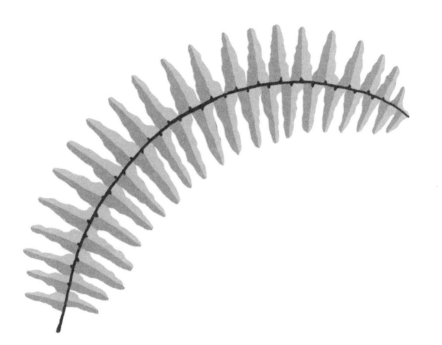

# Xanadu

*Philodendron xanadu*

FAMILY NAME Araceae

CHARACTERISTICS Deeply lobed leaves,
with 15 to 20 lobes, up to 40cm (16in) long

HABITAT Tropical and sub-tropical areas

DISTRIBUTION Tropical USA,
the West Indies and South America

FLOWERS AND FRUIT Flowers have dark-red spathes

The Xanadu plant grows in dense clumps that
spread up to 2 metres (6½ feet) in width, making it
ideal for landscaping in warm climates. This hardy
shrub has serrated leaves with veins that turn a
deep red shade as it matures. Discovered in Western
Australia as a seedling and named *Philodendron*
'Winterbourn', but eventually it was re-named by
House Plants of Australia and called 'Xanadu'. Easy
to grow, the Xanadu has become a popular exotic
foliage plant that thrives inside and out.

# Elkhorn Fern

*Platycerium bifurcatum*

**FAMILY NAME** Polypodiaceae
**CHARACTERISTICS** Evergreen fern with fertile, arching, forked fronds up to 90cm (36in) long, and shorter, sterile, heart-shaped fronds
**HABITAT** Rainforests
**DISTRIBUTION** Native to Australia and New Guinea
**FLOWERS AND FRUIT** Ferns are non-flowering

Also known as Common Staghorn Fern, this plant gets its name from the drooping, forked fronds that resemble a stag's antlers. It has two different types of fronds. Sterile, heart-shaped fronds attach to the trunk or branch of a host tree and act as a support for the rest of the plant; they also catch any debris so that it can be transformed into essential nutrients. Larger, fertile fronds grow from the centre of the first, spreading outwards in a typical 'antler' shape.

# Aspen

*Populus tremuloides*

**FAMILY NAME** Salicaceae

**CHARACTERISTICS** Almost circular 2 to 10cm (¾ to 4in) in length, 2 to 7cm (¾ to 2¾in) width

**HABITAT** Forests, woodlands, thickets, meadows and shrublands

**DISTRIBUTION** Native to North America

**FLOWERS AND FRUIT** The flowers are catkins and appear in early spring. The fruits are a string of capsules, each containing tiny seeds

Also known as the Quaking Aspen or Quaking Poplar, the tree has round leaves that delicately shimmer in the breeze. The leaves twist on the stalk and tremble as the wind passes through them. In autumn they look even more stunning, turning a bright yellow hue. The state tree of Utah, it's also highly popular with beavers, who gnaw through it and use the branches in their lodges. This is a clever choice because the timber doesn't splinter and for this reason is often used to construct benches.

# Douglas Fir

*Pseudotsuga menziesii*

**FAMILY NAME** Pinaceae
**CHARACTERISTICS** Green needles distributed
around each twig, approximately 2.5cm (1in) long
**HABITAT** Prefers slightly acid soils and semi-shade
**DISTRIBUTION** Native to Pacific North America
**FLOWERS AND FRUIT** Male and female flowers grow on the same
tree. Female flowers, once pollinated, develop into oval, hanging cones

These long-lived trees have deep cavities and crevices in
their bark, making them the ideal place for bats and birds
to shelter. Considered a tree of strength by many Native
American tribes, the wood of the Douglas Fir was used to
cover the floor of sweat lodges. All parts of the tree were
utilized – branches were burnt for incense, roots were woven
into baskets and the twigs were made into arrow shafts. Fresh
needle-like leaves are still put to good use and brewed up
in a tea that is rich in vitamin C. Douglas Fir bark is non-
flammable, which protects the trees from forest fires.

# English Oak

*Quercus robur*

**FAMILY NAME** Fagaceae

**CHARACTERISTICS** Green leaves, approximately 10cm (4in) long with 4 to 5 pairs of deep lobes, turning yellow to brown in autumn

**HABITAT** Most common in heavy, wet soils, lowlands, woodlands

**DISTRIBUTION** Most of Europe, parts of China and North America

**FLOWERS AND FRUIT** Only trees over 40 years old produce flowers (yellow catkins) and fruits (acorns)

A common feature in a number of mythologies, the Oak is a powerful symbol of might and endurance. Its Latin name *robur* means 'strength' and it is associated with a wide range of deities from the Greek god of the sky and lightning, Zeus, to his Norse counterpart, Thor, who also governed thunder and lightning. The Celts believed the Oak to be a tree of sacred knowledge and the druids, in particular, would carry out rites and rituals beneath its boughs. Today, the Oak is prized for its hardwood timber and is known to support more wildlife species than any other native tree, from insects to birds to mammals.

# White Willow

*Salix alba*

**FAMILY NAME** Salicaceae
**CHARACTERISTICS** Tapering, slender leaves
5 to 10cm (2 to 4in) long, covered with silky hairs
**HABITAT** Riverbanks
**DISTRIBUTION** Europe, Western and Central Asia
**FLOWERS AND FRUIT** Catkins appear in early spring; once
pollinated they form capsules of tiny seeds dispersed by the wind

With pale, slender leaves covered in downy white hairs, it's easy
to see why the White Willow is so popular with poets and artists.
Though often thought of as a symbol of mourning, it was also a
tree of celebration and its branches were used to decorate churches
on Palm Sunday. Because it grows near water, the tree is associated
with the moon and the Greek moon goddess Hecate. This mystical
link meant that it was commonly thought of as the witch's tree,
because Hecate was known as the Queen of the Witches. Willow
is often coppiced (cut down close to ground level) to produce long,
flexible stems used to weave baskets, furniture and fences.

# Bird of Paradise

*Strelitzia reginae*

FAMILY NAME Strelitziaceae

CHARACTERISTICS Clumps of broadly oblong
leaves up to 70cm (28in) long

HABITAT Riverbanks and shrub clearings near coastal areas

DISTRIBUTION Native to South Africa, also introduced
to Central and Tropical South America

FLOWERS AND FRUITS The exotic flowers are mostly orange
with a touch of blue; fruit is a capsule of small seeds

This striking plant gets its name from the vibrant flowers that resemble the crest of an exotic bird. It's pollinated by sunbirds who rest on the flower's beak-like plinth, triggering a gentle opening of the 'beak' and releasing the pollen. The bird then deposits this on other flowers. This type of pollination, using birds rather than insects, is key to the growth pattern of this plant; as it ages, its flowers get bigger, rather than simply producing more flowers of the same size. Its Latin name *Strelitzia* comes from the amateur botanist Queen Charlotte of Mecklenburg-Strelitz, wife of King George III.

# Rubber Fig

*Ficus elastica*

**FAMILY NAME** Moraceae

**CHARACTERISTICS** Glossy oval leaves, approximately 35cm
(14in) long; ornamental hybrids often have variegated leaves

**HABITAT** Tropical jungle

**DISTRIBUTION** Native from the Himalayas
to Malaysia, Sumatra and Java

**FLOWERS AND FRUIT** Pairs of small yellow-green,
fig-like fruits in its natural habitat

Famous for its milky sap, which was used in the early
1900s to produce a type of rubber, the Rubber Fig
can grow up to 30 metres (100 feet) tall in its native
environment. The leaves, which are broad and
glossy, are much larger on young plants than older
specimens. Pollinated by the fig wasp, it thrives in wet,
humid conditions and enjoys lots of bright sunlight.

# Yew

*Taxus baccata*

FAMILY NAME Taxaceae

CHARACTERISTICS Straight, soft needles grow either
side of the twig, approximately 2.5cm (1in) long

HABITAT A widespread shade species, popular
in parks and gardens, often in churchyards

DISTRIBUTION Europe, Turkey and North Africa

FLOWERS AND FRUIT Tiny male and female flowers borne
on separate trees; female trees bear red berry-shaped fruits (arils)

Sacred to the Druids, this evergreen conifer was associated with the
cycles of life. The Druids respected its longevity and recognized its
ability to regenerate, as mature branches could re-root and form
new trunks if they touched the earth. One of Europe's oldest trees,
the yew is often found in graveyards and has a strong association
with death. Some scholars believe Yews were planted in an effort
to purify plague victims who were buried beneath their branches.
The foliage contains highly poisonous compounds that have been
developed for use in anti-cancer medications.

# Silver Inch Plant

*Tradescantia zebrina*

**FAMILY NAME** Commelinaceae

**CHARACTERISTICS** Fleshy, evergreen, oval or lance-shaped
leaves up to 10cm (4in) long with pointed tips

**HABITAT** Rural and urban areas

**DISTRIBUTION** Native to Mexico,
Central America and Colombia

**FLOWERS AND FRUIT** Small, three-petalled flowers in summer

A species of Spiderwort, Inch Plant stems can grow
around an 25 millimetres (1 inch) every week. New
leaves look purple but eventually turn green, whilst the
underside remains a deep magenta hue. The plant is
also known as the 'Wandering Jew' because of an old
legend about a Jewish man who was cursed to walk the
earth forever. In time the man wandered everywhere,
which is a nod to the abundance of this plant and
its ability to spread rapidly, like the man who
covered the entire earth.

# Spotter's Guide

This leaf checklist will help you identify the 40 leaves in this book. Tick off each leaf as you find it to keep a record. Leaves can be enjoyed in many ways; from the heights of a tall tree or when golden and fallen to the ground. Collect fallen leaves but don't take leaves off plants in the wild.

☐ **Sycamore**
*Acer pseudoplatanus (p8)*

☐ **Asparagus Fern**
*Asparagus setaceus (p16)*

☐ **Begonia**
*Begonia maculata 'Wightii' (p18)*

☐ **Begonia Rex**
*Begonia rex (p20)*

☐ **Silver Maple**

*Acer saccharinum (p10)*

☐ **Horse Chestnut**

*Aesculus hippocastanum (p12)*

☐ **Elephant's Ear**

*Alocasia × amazonica (p14)*

☐ **Silver Birch**

*Betula pendula (p22)*

☐ **Zebra Plant**

*Calathea zebrina (p24)*

☐ **Parlour Palm**

*Chamaedorea elegans (p26)*

☐ **European Fan Palm**

*Chamaerops humilis (p28)*

☐ **Common Hawthorn**

*Crataegus monogyna (p30)*

☐ **Sago Palm**

*Cycas revoluta (p32)*

☐ **Eucalyptus**

*Eucalyptus globulus (p40)*

☐ **Beech**

*Fagus sylvatica (p42)*

☐ **Fittonia**

*Fittonia albivenis (p44)*

☐ **Papyrus**

*Cyperus papyrus (p34)*

☐ **Dumb Cane**

*Dieffenbachia* ssp. *(p36)*

☐ **Areca Palm**

*Dypsis lutescens (p38)*

☐ **Ash**

*Fraxinus excelsior (p46)*

☐ **Ginkgo**

*Ginkgo biloba (p48)*

☐ **Juniper**

*Juniperus communis (p50)*

□ **Honey Locust**

*Gleditsia triacanthos (p52)*

□ **Common Ivy**

*Hedera helix (p54)*

□ **Holly**

*Ilex aquifolium (p56)*

□ **Swiss Cheese Plant**

*Monstera deliciosa (p64)*

□ **Sword Fern**

*Nephrolepis exaltata (p66)*

□ **Xanadu**

*Philodendron xanadu (p68)*

□ **Sweet Gum**

*Liquidambar styraciflua (p58)*

□ **Tulip Tree**

*Liriodendron tulipifera (p60)*

□ **Red-Veined Prayer Plant**

*Maranta leuconeura* var. *erythroneura (p62)*

□ **Elkhorn Fern**

*Platycerium bifurcatum (p70)*

□ **Aspen**

*Populus tremuloides (p72)*

□ **Douglas Fir**

*Pseudotsuga menziesii (p74)*

☐ **English Oak**

*Quercus robur (p76)*

☐ **White Willow**

*Salix alba (p78)*

☐ **Bird of Paradise**

*Strelitzia reginae (p80)*

☐ **Rubber Fig**

*Ficus elastica (p82)*

☐ **Yew**

*Taxus baccata (p84)*

☐ **Silver Inch Plant**

*Tradescantia Zebrina (p86)*

## TOM FROST
### Print Maker

Print maker and illustrator Tom Frost graduated from
Falmouth College of Arts in 2001, returning to his home
town of Bristol to work as an illustrator for a number
of years. He now divides his time between printmaking,
restoring his crumbling Georgian house in rural Wales
and raising a young family. In recent years he has worked
with clients including the V&A, Perry's Cider, Art Angels,
Freight Household Goods, *Selvedge* magazine, Betty &
Dupree, The Archivist and Yorkshire Sculpture Park. His
work highlights a fascination for old matchboxes, stamps,
folk art, tin toys, children's books and the natural world.

**PUBLISHING DIRECTOR** Sarah Lavelle
**CREATIVE DIRECTOR** Helen Lewis
**EDITOR** Harriet Butt
**DESIGNER** Emily Lapworth
**ILLUSTRATOR** Tom Frost
**WORDS** Alison Davies
**PRODUCTION** Vincent Smith,
Nikolaus Ginelli

Quadrille is an imprint of Hardie Grant
www.hardiegrant.com.au

First published in 2017 by
Quadrille Publishing Limited
Pentagon House
52–54 Southwark Street
London SE1 1UN
www.quadrille.co.uk
www.quadrille.com

Cataloguing in Publication Data: A
catalogue record for this book is available
from the British Library.

ISBN 978 1 78713 033 3
Printed in China